The Other

OR

The Project .05: Exploring Ethnic Stereotypes Through the
Production of Five Short Films

INÉS GALIANO

To my parents, for making this project and many other ones possible.

Exploring Ethnic Stereotypes Through the Production of Five
Short Films

_____

A thesis

presented to

the faculty of the Department of Communication

East Tennessee State University

In partial fulfillment

of the requirements for the degree

Masters of Arts in Professional Communication

_____

by

Inés Galiano Torres

May 2016

_____

Shara Lange - Committee Chair

Rustam Sheridan – Committee Member

Wesley Buerkle - Committee Member

Vanessa Mayoraz - Committee Member

Keywords: Ethnic Stereotypes, Film, Television, Media production, New images

INÉS GALIANO

THE OTHER

ABSTRACT

Exploring Ethnic Stereotypes Through the Production of Five

Short Films

by

Inés Galiano Torres

This is a nontraditional thesis that combines social research in

ethnic stereotypes in TV and film with the creative process of

film production. This paper contains the formal step of

research, in addition to the details on the production and

creation of five original short films related to the issue of

ethnic representations.

INÉS GALIANO

TABLE OF CONTENTS

Chapter   Page

ABSTRACT ……………………………………….…..…7

LIST OF FIGURES ……………………………………….12

Chapter

1. INTRODUCTION …………………………………….15

2. LITERATURE REVIEW ……………………………….17

    Stereotypes in Media and Why They Matter……..18

        African American Stereotypes…………………….22

        Latino Stereotypes…………………………………26

        Asian Stereotypes…………………………………32

        Interracial Relationships………………………34

    Perceptions of Media Stereotypes in Other

    Countries………………………………………….38

    Conclusion…………………………………………43

   3. FROM RESEARCH TO PRODUCTION…………………46

    Early Stages……………………………………….46

   4. PRODUCTION…………………………………………53

    FILM I: "What are Stereotypes?" …………………53

        Preproduction……………………………………53

        Production and Postproduction……………………53

    FILM II: "The Mirror" …………………………….55

Preproduction...55

Production...57

Postproduction..59

FILM III: "The Blind Date" 61

Preproduction...61

Production...65

Postproduction..67

FILM IV: "The Show" 68

Preproduction...68

Production...70

Postproduction..72

FILM V: "The Other" 74

Preproduction...74

Production...76

Postproduction..77

5. CONCLUSION..79

Developing My Research...79

Learning About Myself as a Filmmaker and Exploring

the Issue from the Inside...81

Limitations, Progress and Future....................................83

Final Thoughts..86

BIBLIOGRAPHY...89

APPENDICES...95

    Appendix A: Script of "The Blind Date".........................95

    Appendix B: Script of "The Show".............................107

VITA..121

LIST OF FIGURES

Figure   Page

1. Appalachian Student Research Forum..........................46

2. European Scientific Institute...47

3. MIFS, 2015...47

4. Published Paper..48

5. European Scientific Journal Copyright Policies...........48

6. Animation with After Effects..54

7. Production of the "The Mirror"....................................58

8. Color Correction for "The Mirror"...............................59

9. Final version of "The Mirror".......................................60

10. "The Blind Date" Script Excerpt 62

11. First location for "The Blind Date" 63

12. Final location of "The Blind Date" 63

13. Call Sheet...64

14. Production Day...66

15. "The Blind Date" Still..15

16. "The Show" Script Excerpt...69

17. Production of "The Show" 71

18. Caution Sign...72

THE OTHER

19.   Chroma Keying for "The Show".......................73

20. Flyer for the Screening of the Films.................75

21. Screening of the Films and Stereotypes Presentation...77

INÉS GALIANO

THE OTHER

CHAPTER 1

INTRODUCTION

This thesis project is a nontraditional thesis, a combination of social research and film production. Parting from a formal research about representation of ethnic groups through ethnic stereotypes in TV and film, I developed the project and applied my new knowledge into a series of 5 short films in order to further explore the issue.

My main goals during this thesis project were: further develop my research on stereotypes through film production, learn about myself as a filmmaker along the way, and raise awareness about the issue and help make a change happen.

In order to achieve my objectives, I designed a project with a production of 5 short films with different genres; animation, experimental, comical skit, fiction, and documentary. While the first one serves as an introduction to the topic, the last one serves as a conclusion, reflecting on the project and relaying on interviews that bring the project back to social research.

This paper is divided into four main sections: the literature review that was the starting point of my social research, the transition from formal research to production, the production details of the 5 films, and finally, the conclusions and reflections after completing the project.

CHAPTER 2

LITERATURE REVIEW

[This section is taken from Galiano-Torres (2015)]

[1]Audience's Perception of Ethnic Stereotypes in TV shows

Recent research on the portrayals in television of ethnic and cultural groups shows that television is filled with stereotypes depicting these groups. However, further research must be done to determine if these stereotypes produce an effect on the audience. Literature used for this research suggests that television still plays an important role in reinforcing stereotypes. While researching articles written about stereotypes in television, I found several authors that studied the existent mediated stereotypes in television about certain ethnic groups and some others that conducted relevant studies about the stereotypes´ effect on the audience and whose results showed that stereotypes "influence real-world feelings and beliefs about

---

[1] An earlier version of this section was presented at the 3rd Interdisciplinary Forum on Social Sciences and Humanities on 2015, and published in the European Scientific Journal. [Reference to the original paper: Galiano-Torres (2015) in list of references].

these outgroups" (Ramasubramanian 102). These articles provide the starting point for the research questions for this paper about the possible effects on the audience regarding cultural stereotypes in TV shows. The following is a more detailed literature review about this topic divided in different sections: stereotypes in media; African American stereotypes; Latino stereotypes; Asian stereotypes; Interracial relationships; and the study of the issue in other countries. The last section is a projection of what my detailed research questions could be, and what research method would be most appropriate for conducting my study.

Stereotypes in Media and Why they Matter

Much research has focused on the existence of both positive and negative stereotypes in television. The fact is that stereotypes are still present in the media and have several implications for the ethnic and social groups included. Racial or ethnic stereotypes, which are the main topic in this research, are generalizations about an out-group. In this section, we can see some articles focusing on the stereotypes in the media.

THE OTHER

Lee and his colleagues conducted a research on stereotypes as a result of heavy television consumption with college students. Departing from the powerful assumption that; "Positive and negative stereotypes exist in our society" (95), Lee and his colleagues set a study to evaluate the effects of heavy media use in the audience. The study examined the audience's perception of different ethnic groups by means of a voluntary survey. Their findings showed that heavy television consumers perceived more negative stereotypes and that Caucasians were the group associated the least with these negative stereotypes (107). There was also a difference between television genres, since "heavy viewers of entertainment, educational and sports program appeared to have more negative ethnic perceptions" (107), while viewers of information programming, such as news, had more positive perceptions. Their results support the idea of the media having an impact on the audience's perception, which has several implications; there is a need a more active role on how the media educates society. Lee and his colleagues state that, considering the amount of influence the media have on consumers, consumers should be educated to question the information given, and that scholars can "encourage media critique as well as promote efforts to reduce stereotypical portrayals" (108).

Ramasubramanian´s study on television viewing and racial attitudes also explores the perception of White viewers about other ethnic groups, especially African-Americans and Latino-Americans, and the influence on their beliefs about these groups. In his words, "television has a history of underrepresenting, marginalizing, and caricaturing non-White characters" (103). Stereotypical portrayals in television of these groups on television are considered to contribute to negative stereotyping, because these groups are depicted as "different, inferior, and'othered'" (Ramasubramanian 104).

Ramasubramanian's findings suggest that stereotypes influence negative feelings toward ethnic groups; in his research, African-American and Latino-American groups were associated with criminality and laziness. As we can extract from both articles, television is still an influential medium for reinforcing racial attitudes and opinions.

But how about the content created by the viewers themselves? Guo and Harlow conducted a content analysis regarding Youtube videos containing stereotypes of Black, Latino and Asians. Departing from the Youtube´s motto "Broadcast yourself", they expected to find alternative media. For their analysis, they watched 150 Youtube's most-viewed videos about each ethnic group (Blacks, Latinos, and Asians). They were trying to find how "racial stereotypes were treated in the Youtube videos" (2). In order to do so, they coded the videos as reinforcing (if they showed the stereotypes as true), or as challenging (if they showed nonstereotypical images). The common stereotypes they coded in the videos were "law breaker", "uneducated", "poor", "rapper" for Black people. The most common stereotypes for Latino coded were "law breaker", "uneducated", "poor", "illegal immigrant" and "sexualized women". Asian stereotypes coded were "model minority", "hard-working", "business oriented", "nerdy" and "sexualized women". Their results showed that videos related to Black stereotypes were challenging them more than the other videos regarding the other races (45%). Latino videos, however, where the less challenging (2%). The most common stereotype portrayed for the different ethnic groups was "lawbreaker" for Blacks, "sexualized women" for Latino and "nerd physical appeareance and language pronunciation" for Asians (291). The analysis showed that individuals, not companies or professional organizations, uploaded 86 % of the videos. The authors found also that videos with stereotypes had more views than videos without stereotypes. Finally, their results supported that the majority of videos (85%) were reinforcing racial stereotypes, while just a few were challenging them. Their study suggests that even user-generated Youtube's videos support the "racial hierarchy as emphasized in the mainstream media" (299).

As we can infer from what the articles propose, stereotypes are present in television, whether they are positive or negative. The existence of stereotypes composes a mainstream generalized view about a specific group. Our last article proofs that not only the mainstream media produce stereotypes, but also the consumers; even consumer-generated videos are full of ethnic stereotypes.

African American Stereotypes

After stating the importance of stereotypes, I will focus on specific examples of stereotyped ethnic groups or stereotype's research. The present section will deal with the existence of African American Stereotypes in television and how this group is portrayed, as well as the implications that the stereotypes have for the audience.

Northup conducted a study on implicit and explicit attitudes toward African Americans using Cultivation Theory as a framework. The author states that media can have an important role in maintaining and creating the dominant culture: in this case, the negative attitudes towards African-Americans (29). In his research, Northup was testing the differences between heavy viewers of television and light viewers in their perceptions of African Americans. He used a quantitative method based on surveys conducted after watching a piece of news. This piece of news was different for two different groups: in one group, participants were exposed to an African American suspect, while in the other group, participants were exposed to a Caucasian suspect. Participants were surveyed about the level of guilt the would assign to the suspect as well as some other demographic questions to evaluate the amount of media watched by the participant. The results of the study are highly interesting in relation to the present research, since they showed that those participants who were heavy viewers thought the African American suspect was guiltier than the light viewers (22). The clearly different level of guilt assigned by the two types of participants was compared with the almost no difference shown between heavy viewers and light viewers when assigning a level of guilt to the Caucasian suspect. In both groups, the piece of news was contained the same information, with the only difference being the picture of the Caucasian suspect or the African American suspect. Therefore, as Northup points out that, a heavy consumption of media has an influence in the audience´s attitudes towards African Americans, since the media´s criminal portrayals of this ethnic group are higher. According to Northup, findings show the potential damage of a high use of criminal stereotypes by the media: "If new users are trained to believe that an African American they see is guilty, then the entire justice system could be undermined" (38).

These mediated stereotypes also affect the stereotyped ethnic group. Sanders and Ramasubramanian conducted further research on the audience's perception of the stereotypes when the audience itself belonged to the stereotyped group. According to the researchers, viewers of television shows exposed to limited depictions of some groups were influenced and would categorize these groups. Categorization is the maximization of differences between social groups and minimization between group members, creating an "us" and "them" perspective (Sanders and Ramasubramanian 19). While

recent research has focused on the non- minority audience's
perception of the various ethnic groups in relation with the
judgments the audience makes, this study has centered in the
presentation of stereotypical depictions of different ethnic
groups to the stereotyped groups, specially African Americans.
Sanders and Ramasubramanian conducted a study by means of
an online survey with 154 African American participants
regarding their perceptions of 30 fictional media characters,
such as Hispanics, African Americans and Asian Americans.
Participants were asked to describe the characters by choosing
among the adjectives they were given. The results showed that
perceptions of African American characters were favorable,
while the support for the other groups was mixed. Therefore,
Sanders and Ramasubramanian come to the conclusion that
ethnic groups do not have the same perception of themselves
that Caucasians have about them, although there is still the
media's impact in how the groups think about one another (35).
Their study is highly important because it corroborates the
media's ability to affect the audience's emotions towards
different ethnic groups from their own, but it does not have an
effect on the stereotyped group itself.

We can see that African American stereotypes still exist in

the media and that they have an influence in the audience with possible implications. African American stereotypes found in research include images such as the aggressive figure.

Latino Stereotypes

Similar to the previous section, this sections deals with Latino stereotypes in the media and how they impact the audience. Some studies start to show a difference in tendencies towards stereotypes, although they are still present in primetime television. In this regard, Mastro and Morawitz conducted a content analysis of the television representation of the largest ethnic minority group in the United States, which is Latino (12.5%). Departing from the fact that former content analysis have found Latino characters being depicted as stereotypic and often with negative characterizations, including "the criminal, the law enforcer, the Latin Lover, the Harlot, and the comic/buffoon" (111). Following the frame of Cultivation Theory, a heavy exposure to television changes viewers perceptions, which means that learning from television's depictions of Latinos could influence interactions in real life.

Mastro and Morawitz's findings in their study showed that, in a two-week television programming on the most popular networks, Latinos only represented 3.9% of characters, which is highly underrepresented, compared to the actual population, and they were not likely interact with white peers. They had lower job authority, but the tendency to depict them as subordinate was decreasing. They were generally thin and attractive, depicting them as "additively romantic, sensual, sexual, and even exotically dangerous" (125). Latinos were also depicted as least intelligent and articulate, the laziest, and most verbally aggressive. Therefore, Mastro and Morawitz get to the conclussion that, ethnicity "does, in fact, impact the manner in which characters are depicted on primetime television" (124) and, although there are improvements over previous decades, stereotypes persist.

Merskin also investigates the perpetuation of the stereotypes in television. Her study is focused on the hot-latina stereotype. Merskin conducts a textual analysis of the show *Desperate Housewives*. Although a Latino character as a lead character is not usual, the hispanic character Gabrielle Solis plays an important role in the show, which at first can be seen as an achievement. However, Merkin's study shows that the depiction of Gabrielle´s character during several episodes is still filled with the usual behavior that belongs to the female hispanic or latina stereotype. Gabrielle Solis and even the actress in real life, Eva Longoria, appear often in the show and in magazines in a way that reinforces the "prominent, oversexed, under-dressed" latina character (Merskin 134). According to Merkin, beliefs about race, ethnicity, sex and gender are reinforced through television and "an ideology of White/Anglo racial superiority is maintained by using stereotypes" (134). She also states that stereotypes "reduce individuals to a single, monolithic, one-dimensional type that appears and is presented as natural and normal" (135). In her article, she suggests that stereotypes become naturalized through their repetition and support cultural beliefs and values about certain groups of people based on distorted presentations of qualities, which increases the sense of the "other".

Avila-Saavedra studies also the Latino stereotypes in television, but focuses on the Identity of Latinos in the U.S. In his research, he analyzed Latino television comedies that "articulate an implicit tension between ethnic otherness and desire for assimilation for U.S. Latinos" (271). Three comedies are analyzed exploring the Latino identity and how media legitimates or defies cultural perceptions: *George Lopez, Freddie,* and *Mind of Mencia*. He found that Latino comedy shows are full of ethnic insults that on the one hand, "is an explicit articulation of cultural otherness", and, on the other hand "it makes the joke acceptable for Latino and non-Latino audiences" (282), in an effort to be included in U.S. mainstream culture. Latino comedians affirm their otherness by ridiculing themselves and non-Latinos, in order to "provide relief for the accumulated tensions that originate from Latinos´ self-perceived lower social status. In any form of struggle for social power, a desire to challenge dominant values competes with a desire to become part of the dominant ideology" (286). The comic content requires adaptation, since it has references to U.S. history and culture, making it Latino comedy for U.S. Latinos, not for Latin Americans. The use of Latino stereotypes confirms the Latino ethnic identity, but also the inclusion in American mainstream. These comedies are popular among U.S. Latinos for identity construction and among the non-Latino audience as a new source of information about Latinos that embrace U.S. values, which ease social fears (289).

Mastro and Tukachinsky, however, look at the issue from a different perspective. Their study is based on media´s depictions of good stereotypes and the possible good effects that these can have in the White audience, regarding their possible improved judgment of the stereotyped groups. The authors conducted a triple study in which they looked for the effect on the audience after being exposed to favorable Latino depictions. They exposed the participants in the first study to a well-liked Latino actor and then their evaluations of Latinos were analyzed. In the second study, they showed a group of Latino portrayed favorably in a television show, and in the third study, a mixture of the group and the picture. Their hypothesis was that the audience's evaluations would be more favorable after the exposure. The results of their study suggested that the depiction of favorable stereotypes has an effect on the audience regarding their evaluation of ethnic groups. Their findings showed that the exposed audience was more likely to give a generous evaluation of the group. Their study also showed that to reduce the negative stereotypes is not enough to affect the audience but there is a need for the inclusion of favorable or counterstereotypical data. However, their findings also suggested that an "extreme disconfirmation of the stereotype is likely to overly challenge audience members' existing views leading to dismissal of the information as too deviant" (933).

Their conclusion is to increase favorable media depiction of these ethnic groups, but also adding audience´s preexisting cognitions, such as positive stereotypes.

Murillo and Escala conducted a study on the popular television show *Ugly Betty*, examining the transformations of the media constructions of the Latino population in the US, providing a more complex cultural portrayal. The character of Betty Suarez, tries to attract the people in her community representing the Latina stereotype, but also, having a Latino character as the main character is a novelty in the Latino excluded television world. According to the authors, *Ugly Betty* is an example of how culture is represented and the meaning constructed through the characters of television shows, and their qualities and representations. Betty is a character in a context in which others (White Americans) perceive her as foreign and different; not only someone ugly, but someone that does not belong in the culture. The television show, however, after proposing the social exclusion issue, proposes also a solution through the acceptance of multiculturalism in the US. Betty will fight for being accepted, while conserving her culture and family values. Her final transformation, more than being a physical change, it is also a social and cultural change. When she is accepted and she achieves integration in society, the television show depicts a world in which difference is possible. This television drama, produced by the Latina actress Salma Hayek, it is a proposal of a social project; a representation of exclusion methods and possibilities of inclusion of the Latino population in the United States.

Latino stereotypes have been extensively researched, as well as African American stereotypes. We still find the existence of Latino stereotypes in the media, increasingly even due to the current growth of this population. Latino stereotypes found are several, such as the passionate Latin Lover or Hot Latina, and the aggressive *bandido*.

Asian Stereotypes

This section will deal with Asian American stereotypes, even it they have not been extensively researched. However, the scarce existent research is highly relevant. Here a single article is depicted:

Asian Americans have also been stereotyped, as we can see

in Zhang's study on the impact of stereotypes on the interactions between Asians and non-Asians. Applying also from Cultivation theory and the presence of stereotypical characters in media, Zhang tested different hypothesis on how Asian Americans will be perceived. The hypothesis were that they will be perceived as more likely "to achieve academic success" (Zhang 25), "to be perceived as nerds" (26), "to be left out" (27), and peers will be "less likely to initiate friendship with Asian Americans" (27). Zhang constructed four scenarios for her research and asked the participants to read them and respond a survey afterwards. For instance, in the first scenario, Jane was a student with a perfect GPA who had won various math contests. Participants were asked to rate if they thought Jane was "Asian, Black, Hispanic or White" (29). After having participants read the four scenarios and answer similar questions, Zhang's findings showed that Asians were rated "the highest in academic achievement" (30), "the highest in the lack of social skills" (31), "the highest in peer rejection" (31), and that "the likelihood to initiate friendship with Asians was found to score the lowest" (31). Zhang's results demonstrated that Asians are perceived "as nerds who are intelligent, hardworking, and technologically talented but clumsy and lacking appropriate social and communication skills" (32), exactly as the Asian stereotype. People´s judgments of Asians are influenced by ethnic stereotypes, and they affect the interactions between this groups and other groups.

Although there is a need for research focusing on this ethnic group, we can still find stereotypes such as the hard-working or nerdy figure, which confirms that Asian Americans are also a stereotyped ethnic group in television.

Interracial Relationships

Finally, another research matter is the representation of stereotyped interracial relationships that include current racial stereotypes. As in the case of Asian American stereotypes, it is not an extended topic for research, so I will just mention one article.

In her article, Washington studies the depiction of interracial relationships in television. Specifically, the author looks at the relationship between the Black and the Asian characters of the popular television dramas *Grey´s Anatomy* and

ER, regarding the representation of interracial relationships from a hegemonic point of view. Washington argues that much research on interracial relationships has been done with Black and White, Latino and White or Asian and White, but not much among the non-hegemonic ethnic groups, such as Black and Latino or Asian and Black. These representations, although they reflect the change in times towards a multicultural society, depict the traditional stereotyped Black male and the traditional Asian female, and "reproduce power relations that support the White privileged racial hegemony" (256). Under a label of *color-neutral* or *color-blind* and including more and more ethnic characters in television, "Whites avoid being labeled racist" but representations of race are still stereotypical and their stories are told from the White hegemonic narrative perspective (258). In the analyzed television show *Grey's Anatomy,* the character of Cristina Yang represents the stereotype of the "dragon lady" (the hypersexualized lady with fiery temperament), she is brilliant in her work and aggressive, and she seems unable to control her sexual desire (259). The opposing stereotype is the "lotus blossom" (a virginal, submissive young woman). This stereotype is represented in the second analyzed show *ER,* with the characters of Jing-Mei Chen and Neela Rasgotra. Both dramas show how "Asian Americans should conduct themselves in order to fit into White Society" (260). They should be brilliant, either hypersexual or virginal, and they should not complain about the hard work. On the other hand, the Black male characters who they are paired with in the shows, represent also the two Black stereotypes: the "tom" (the submissive, kind and selfless) and the "brutal black buck", oversexed and dangerous (260). The representation of the tom is used to "remind Blacks that they need only to obey their White 'masters' to solve all their problems" (260). The character Dr. Burke, who is paired with the furious Cristina Yang, is the representation of the tom in *Grey's Anatomy*. He never gets angry and remains loyal to the; he is extremely kind and even dies for his country. Finally, the relationship between the stereotyped Asian females and Black males is depicted either as a marriage without sex, like Rasgotra and Gallant's relationship, or as a "sexual relationship that cannot lead to marriage", like Yang and Burke's relationship or Chen and Prat's relationship. It is worth mentioning that Dr Chen's character had had a previous interracial relationship with a Black male that ended in a multicultural baby that she gave up for adoption. This representation "addresses popular culture's discomfort with multiracial people" (266), and the audience is not shown what a multiracial baby could bring to the "color-neutral" world of *ER*. A similar case happens in *Grey's Anatomy* when Yang gets pregnant and she has a miscarriage. Yang and Burke's relationship ends up when Burke leaves her at the altar: the hierarchies remain (264). As a conclusion, Washington argues that the depiction of Asian females and Black males in relationships in television "as examples of attempt at resisting the dominant hegemony, these shows are doing the opposite by playing directly into the racial hierarchy" (265), since they are dramatic and have a tragic end: the children that they could have, are either eliminated (miscarriage) or silenced (adoption). These television shows, according to the author are of highly importance because they construct cultural symbols, and these representations do not challenge the stereotypes or try to understand Asian or Black people. In addition, while this troubled interracial relationships are represented, "Whiteness maintains its position at the top of the hierarchy". As we can see in this article, interracial relationships are also stereotyped and represented in a way that favors the hegemonic dominant view, still increasing the importance of the hierarchy.

INÉS GALIANO

Perceptions of Media Stereotypes in Other Countries

The issue of the effect of mediated stereotypes on the audience and how to promote a different media strategy have also been addressed in other countries. Therefore, even though the common stereotypes will be different in other cultures, the fact that the issue is also relevant in other countries makes this problem become important worldwide.

Igartua, Barrios and Ortega address this issue focusing on prime-time television in Spain. Their study focuses on depictions of immigrants on television entertainment produced in Spain. Immigration increased highly in Spain in the last few years, and immigrants now consist of the 12.2% of the population, accompanied by xenophobic reactions and attitudes towards immigrants (6). In order to evaluate the media representations of immigrants groups Igartua, Barrios and Ortega conducted a content analysis of the characters that appeared in Spanish fiction in television. Their hypothesis were to find an underrepresentation of immigrant characters compared to native characters, as it is found in the United States television shows (e.g. 3.9% of Latino characters, while this group comprise the 12.5% of the population in United States); immigrants characters occupying a higher level of secondary roles and/or antagonists roles than native; and a lower socio-economic level and lower level of education is shown among immigrants characters. For the analysis, two full weeks of prime-time programming were selected randomly and recorded, but only fictional programs were analyzed. Although only 19.3% of the shows were actually produced in Spain (versus the 71.6% of shows produced in the United States), they focused on the Spain-produced programs for the study. Results of the study showed that there was in fact an underrepresentation of immigrants characters (7.8% of characters were immigrants, although there is a 12.2% of immigrant population in Spain); the immigrant characters were depicted with a lower educational and job level, and a higher violent behavior. According to Igartua, Barrios and Ortega, media's depictions of foreigners may "strengthen or foment prejudicial attitudes towards immigrants" (22). This study allows us to see the expansion of the issue in other countries where different ethnic or cultural groups are in contact.

Inzunza-Acedo also conducted research to determine the audience's perception of stereotypes in television, by analyzing the fans' reception of the television show *Lost* with focus groups in Mexico. The selection of the show was due to the multicultural variety of its characters, since they are from diverse origin such as American, Hispanic, European and Asian. After conducting the study, the results indicated that several stereotypes were reinforced. Inzunza-Acedo suggests that the lead character, Jack, of Caucasian origin, represented the perfect American hero and the audience admired him (23). His antagonist and also Caucasian, Sawyer, who is depicted at first as the villain but later as a secondary hero, invents nicknames for the rest of the characters that reinforce the stereotypical idea that they represent. When it comes to non-Caucasian characters, however, they are no longer depicted in the role of the hero. First, Inzunza-Acedo determined that the Hispanic characters were depicted as fat and naive in the case of one male character, Hurley, and as rude and aggressive in the case of two female characters, Ana Lucía and Ilana. The audience liked Hurley and disliked the two female Hispanic characters. Second, Merskin found that the European characters in the show were depicted as dirty and crazy, (e.g. the French character named Rousseau), extremely romantic, (e.g. the Scottish character Desmond), and drug abusers, (e.g. the British character Charlie). Third, the Asian characters were depicted as highly traditional:

the female Asian character, Sun, is completely submissive to her husband Jin, a male Asian character. These characters are isolated from the rest of the group until they start their westernization: they learn English and she acts more liberally. The audience thought this depiction of the two characters was completely normal, and participants even affirmed that "Asian people were like that" (Merskin 25). The African-American character, Michael, was depicted as skilled in manual work; and the African character, a Nigerian named Eko, depicted as stubborn and wild. The audience felt indifference for both of them. Finally, the Middle East character, and Iraqi named Sayid, is a veteran specialized in torture, and is perceived by the audience as the "terrorist" (25). Inzunza-Acedo's analysis of the characters suggests that all characters are stereotyped according to the culture that they belong to and that there is a sense of superiority in the Caucasian characters compared to the rest of cultures and nationalities. These stereotypes are not only promoted but also validated by comical situations that please the audience.

Another article on the issue has been conducted in Norway, with Halse's study on the audience's perceptions of the portrayal of a Muslim family in the action show *24.* According to

Halse, the traditional Muslim stereotype has been constructed on a 'Middle East' image the Muslim Arab-American, and *24* has contributed to the promotion of this stereotype. This portrayal of a character is always related to terrorism, even if the character is integrated in the neighborhood and lives an ordinary life in the United States. Halse conducted his research by means of recording and identifying attitudes through focus groups interviews. Five of the seven focus groups consisted of young adults from a secondary school, while two groups of participants were Muslims immigrants from an Immigrant Education Centre. Selected scenes regarding this terrorist family from the show were screened, and they were asked about their perceptions of the characters. Norwegians participants tend to expressed more excitement and found the show more entertaining than the Muslim participants, who actually found it unpleasant and offensive. Norwegians tended to associate the Muslims as "the foreigners", while the Muslims participants tended to see "Americans" as responsible for the offense in the show. From the study's results, Halse states that "texts like *24*'s can function as stimuli for interpretive communities in the negotiation of boundaries between us and them" (49) and that "the new Muslim stereotype, in addition to eliciting insecurity and xenophobia among non-Muslims, is also troubling for the Muslim immigrant community" (49). Halse´s findings have serious implications, since the proposed stereotype is no longer innocent or funny, but have a secret violent desire to attack and destroy Western life, which certainly leads to a negative and discriminatory attitude towards, and from, Muslims, and deteriorate the environment in which these two cultures have contact.

These articles demonstrate that the study of stereotypes is a new but increasing research topic in other countries and cultures, outside the US. The stereotypes found in the articles are, however, similar to the ones found in the research articles in the US.

Conclusion

The repeated depiction of cultural stereotypes in television shows reinforces and validates the notion of the "other." The articles reviewed for this research provide the most relevant findings regarding this issue. However, further research needs to be done to determine the possible effects on the audience and changes in attitudes towards different cultural or ethnic groups after the exposure to these stereotypes and how the effects could impact real-life interactions among different groups.

From the literature review, we can see the vast amount of research conducted around the depictions and representations of ethnic groups in television. However, not much has been done around the perceptions of the audience and the impact that these perceptions have in real life. It is true that measuring the impact in society is a difficult task, but conducting research to prove that there is in fact an influence or that there is not, it is important to help determine if there is a need for change. If research proves and supports the evidences of a negative influence in the audience after the heavy consumption of stereotyped content, it would be highly possible that these acquired beliefs will play a role when encountering people from these stereotyped ethnic groups. If the negative effect is proven, then there is a need for change in television representation. Television representations that provide tools and promote discrimination should not be encouraged or tolerated. Also, possible measures against stereotypical content or the promotion of counterstereotypical content should be studied, which is why conducting further research on the audience´s perceptions of biased television ethnic representations is vitally important.

CHAPTER 3

FROM RESEARCH TO PRODUCTION

Early Stages

The previous literature review represented the very first step into this thesis project. I wrote it as a research paper under the supervision of Dr. Buerkle for one of the classes of the Masters Program. Later on, I decided to present at the Appalachian Student Research Forum at East Tennessee State University in Spring 2015 (see Figure 1.)

Figure 1. Appalachian Student Research Forum
(Photo Credit: Yohann Aboa)

It was a great experience for me, so I decided to submit my paper to another conference in Barcelona: The 3ʳᵈ Mediterranean Interdisciplinary Forum on Social Sciences and Humanities, MIFS, 2015, organized by the European Scientific Institute (see Figure 2.) I got my paper accepted, I presented at the Forum (see Figure 3), and my research paper was published in the European Scientific Journal under a Creative Commons License, meaning that I still retain the copyright of the work and the publishing rights (see Figure 4 and 5.)

Figure 2. European Scientific Institute

Figure 3. MIFS, 2015

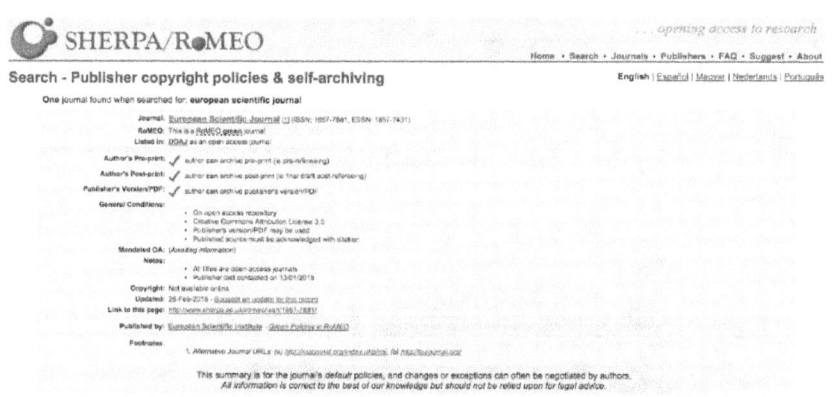

European Scientific Journal July 2015 /SPECIAL/ edition ISSN: 1857 – 7881 (Print) e - ISSN 1857- 7431

AUDIENCE'S PERCEPTION OF CULTURAL/ETHNIC STEREOTYPES IN TV SHOWS

Inés Galiano Torres, Current MA Student
East Tennessee State University, USA

Figure 4. Published Paper

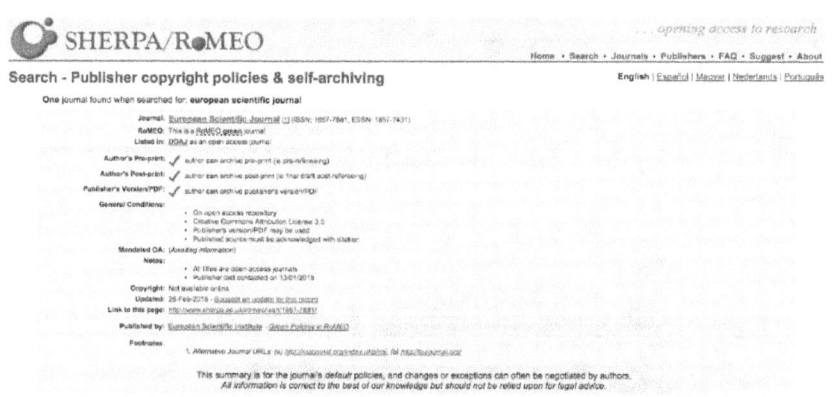

Figure 5. European Scientific Journal Copyright Policies

Presenting at both conferences was a really important

learning experience for me, but I decided that I wanted to create a more hands on project for my thesis. Since my concentration is Radio-Television-Film, I decided to make a series of film based on what I had researched. I designed a Production Thesis Project, which would allow me to keep researching this topic but in a nontraditional way, allowing me to improve my production and filmmaking skills at the same time.

Addressing Stereotypes in television could be approached in many different ways, but I decided to approach it via filmmaking. In order to understand better how the industry works, I wanted to try to produce myself a body of work about the topic. Filmmaking has some virtues and limitations, like any other approach. The main virtue that this approach offered me is that it is a more empirical and hands on form, and I could express much through it. However, it also has some limitations, including that it may not always be as direct as other approaches and that it may not be as generalizable.

Also, trying to develop the formal research into production had some challenges, since there are certain conflicts between studying media and making films. When studying media, we can actually stop to think about the reasons behind it and the symbols that come with a film, even if that may not be the original idea when the film was being produced. However, in Film Production, drama and the story beats are important, and sometimes they may have the same level of importance that the message that is being passed across. While trying to write drama and trying to engage the audience, writers can forget about the symbols and original intended message, if there is a message at all.

With all this in mind, I decided to choose the filmmaking approach, because It would allow me to explore the issue from the origin of it (the production of stereotypes in film) and it would allow me to grow as a filmmaker. I designed a 5-film project. One of the main ideas behind the design of 5 different films was the opportunity to be able to try different genres and get some experience and skills working with all of them. This is the original detailed list of films that I designed:

1. Animation Short Film: It will work as an introduction to the topic of Stereotypes. It will be a stop motion made in Photoshop and animated through After Effects, with infographics and research

data from the literature research conducted previously. Duration of this film: Around 1 minute.

2. Experimental Film: A nightmare that the main character has. Original script based on the fears of the character. Duration of this film: Around 2 minutes.

3. Comedy Skit. Short situational comedy scene about the interaction between a Hispanic character and a non-Hispanic character on a first date. Duration of this film: Around 3 minutes.

4. Metafilm: A short fiction film about the production of a low budget telenovela, and how the stereotypes are created for the screen. Duration: Around 5 minutes.

5. Documentary: Making-of and behind the scenes of the process, research and production of this thesis project, in addition to the reactions of audiences to the film and topic. Duration of this film: Around 10 minutes.

It must be noted that, having almost no experience in Film Production, this was not only an ambitious project but also a learning challenge for me. With that in mind, I decided to improve my production skills and enrolled in a one-month intensive summer workshop at Prague Film School, during the month of June 2015. At the workshop, I learned basic film production skills that would be so helpful later on during the production of this thesis project. I made an effort to learn as much as possible and I ended up winning the Audience Award at the final workshop screening. I was ready to start.

CHAPTER 4

PRODUCTION

Film I: "What are Stereotypes?"

Preproduction

This first film was designed as introduction to the topic of stereotypes for the audience. I chose to do animation, since I thought it would be more visually attractive than other kinds of images. The writing of the script was simple; I just pulled the main ideas from the research I had conducted previously on the topic. I decided that this first film would have a duration of 1 minute for two main reasons: the first one, being that my animation skills were still developing and animation takes patience, time and several years of practice; the second one was that the audience's attention span for this kind of informational videos is rather limited. For both reasons, one minute seemed to be the best option for this first introductory film.

Production and Postproduction

Since the animation was completely developed in the computer, these two steps (usually two separate steps in film production), were combined. For this video, I created several images in different software, such as Photoshop; and then I made the animation in After Effects (see Figure 6), animating frame by frame every image and layer to introduce the movement. I did have to learn and improve my After Effects skills, which I managed through online tutorials step by step.

The final duration of this film is 1 minute and seven seconds, and it uses creative commons music from Jamendo, a website with free license music.

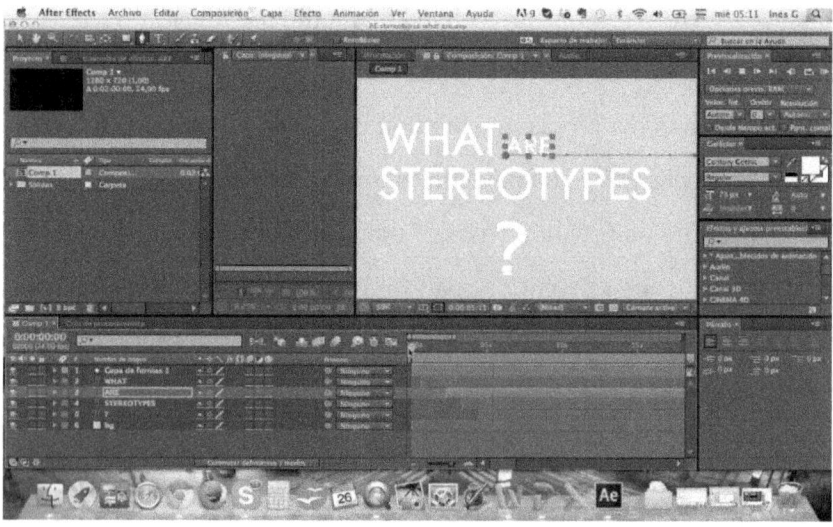

Figure 6. Animation with After Effects. (Computer Screenshot)

Film II: "The Mirror"

Preproduction

For this film, I chose to try the experimental genre and to make a short film of about two minutes. The main idea behind this film is self-representation and perception when it comes to people from different ethnicities. I had this in mind when I wrote a script about three women (an Asian one, a Latina, and a European one), who are looking at themselves in the mirror. The three of them make the exact same movements, that way representing how much they are alike; but with the use of different color filters and objects that will represent how society sees them differently.

The plot of this film is simple: three women, that completely embraced their ethnic stereotype, decide to remove their clothes, jewerely, make up and wash their face, as a symbol of removing the society standards to finally be who you really are. I chose female roles because it is my belief that women suffer the most when it comes to society standards and stereotypes.

For the Latina girl I chose the red color, because it is a

common misconception that Latinos are passionate and hot-tempered. Thus, red was the perfect color for my character. She had to wear a red dress and the objects in the bathroom should be red. I looked for red towels and red hand soap, and I found a red screen to use over the lights to give a red tone to the whole scene.

In the same way, I used the color yellow for my Asian character; she wore a yellow shirt and used yellow objects, and the color blue for the European one; she wore a blue dress and used a blue towel.

Being the Vice President of the International Student Association at East Tennessee State University, I had no problems finding the international cast I needed for this film. The three chosen actresses for these roles were: Maria Aparcero, Rei Mitsushio and Juliette Guerrault. The three of them ended up being casted again in my following films.

In order to prepare for this film as much as possible, I not only wrote the script, but also a shot list that would make the production run more smoothly. I rented the equipment from the RTVF equipment room: a Blackmagic Pocket camera and a light kit with colored filters. I used my own camera to get behind the scenes footage.

Production

The production schedule for this film was one day only, since this film was going to have duration of around two minutes. The location for this film was my own bathroom in my apartment, which is not really big, so there were some issues trying to set up the lights (see Figure 7.)

The cast was ready early in the morning and we started shooting by 11 A.M. The production run really smoothly, considering this was the first film that I was actually shooting and that some of the cast members were fairly new to acting. We had a lunch break, during which I cooked homemade pasta for the cast, since one of the things I learned in film school is that the most important thing to do, even in low budget films, is to feed the cast and crew.

Using the different colors in the bathroom made the production slower, since we had to change the different objects and the colored filters every time. I also was the only member in the crew, and I think it would have been easier if I had had some help, since I had to ask for help to the same actresses for small tasks such as holding the reflector. However, overall, the production was smooth and without major problems.

Figure 7. Production of the "The Mirror" (Stationary camera)

Postproduction

The post-production was the most complicated part of this film, with no doubts. Being my first experience with the experimental genre, I really did not know what to expect or how to approach the post-production. I had to do several drafts and rough cuts, changing everything every time, until we got to the point where my advisor and me were satisfied with the result. Being experimental, the goal was not to create the most beautiful film, but to create the most creative or original possible (see Figure 8.)

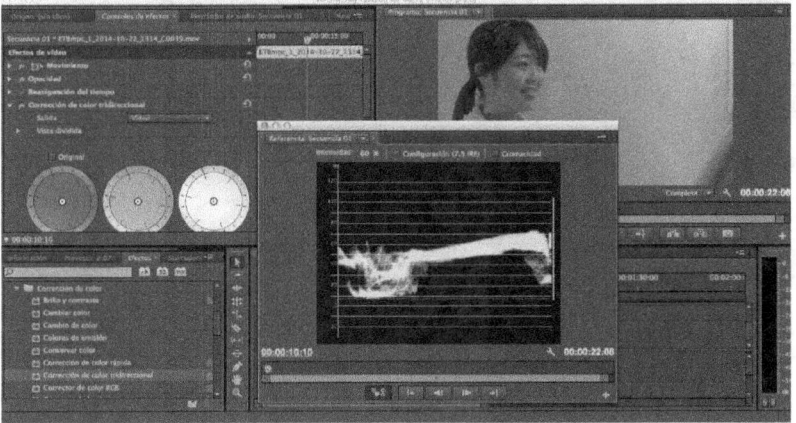

Figure 8. Color Correction for "The Mirror"

Playing with different editing filters in the software editing program that I used to edit this film (Adobe Premiere Pro), I finally developed the idea of the image split in half (see Figure 9.) The characters are looking at themselves in the mirror and the reality of the mirror may not be the same that outside of it. With that idea in mind, it made sense for me to split my image in half and have a different colored shot in each side. I finally came up with an edited version that was experimental and also passed the message across easily. The music was also free license music from the website Jamendo. The final duration of the film is 2 minutes and 7 seconds.

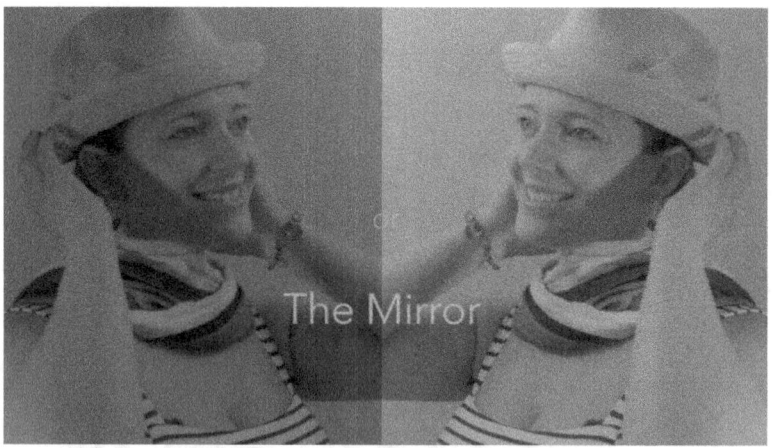

Figure 9. Final version of "The mirror"

Film III. "The Blind Date"

Preproduction

The genre that I chose for this film was a comedy Skit. The main plot would be a short situational comedy scene about the interaction between a Hispanic character and a non-Hispanic character on a first date. I started to write the script and look for casting at the same time, so when I decided that I would work with Juliette again for this film; I modified the script to include not only the Hispanic stereotypes but also the French stereotypes (see Figure 10.)

In this film, Juliette plays the role of a supposedly French girl that is in love with the Latin lover stereotype and brings her ideas of what a Latino man should be to her Blind Date. On the other hand, Yoel Martinez plays the role of a supposedly Mexican boy who is expecting Juliette to be the stereotypical French person. There is a dialogue full of French and Mexican symbols, until they both realize that they are not what they thought at first.

```
                    WAITRESS
               What can I get for you?

They split suddenly, embarrassed.

                     YOEL
               Cavernet Sauvignon.

                   JULIETTE
               Cerveza Modelo.

Waitress writes quickly and disappears.


They look at each other. They are nervous, trying not to
look at each other.

                    JULIETTE
           So... what type of music do you like?

                     YOEL
               I love Piaf, Edith Piaf.

                    JULIETTE
           Oh wow... one of the classics...

                      YOEL
                And you?

                    JULIETTE
             I love Enrique Iglesias!
```

Figure 10. "The Blind Date" Script Excerpt

I also rented the equipment from the RTVF equipment
room at ETSU. I rented the BlackMagic Pocket camera again, the
audio Zoom recorder, and a boom microphone and pole. For the
location, at first I thought that the backyard of my house would
work to make it more satirical, and there was actually a first
version of the film that was shot in there (see Figure 11.)
However, after editing the film, it became clear that there was a
need for a better location for the film, to make it look more

professional. That location ended up being the Mexican Restaurant El Charolais, that is located near ETSU (see Figure 12.) The owner was kind enough to let us shoot at the restaurant in the hours before opening at no cost.

Figure 11. First location for "The Blind Date" (Stationary Camera)

Figure 12. Final location of "The Blind Date" (Film Still)

Some RTVF students volunteered as Crew members for the shoot, and I prepared a Call Sheet that I sent to them beforehand (see Figure 13.) This time I had a cinematographer, an audio operator and Assistant Director.

CALL SHEET Date: Saturday, October 14th
Shoot Day: 1
Shoot Call: 1

TITLE: 3 or The Blind Date   PRODUCER: RTVF PCOM

PROJECT #:   3   DIRECTOR: Ines Galiano

SET/SCENE DESCRIPTION	SCENE	CAST	DAY/NIGHT	PGS	LOCATION
INT. SCENE 1	1 A	1,2	DAY	6	El Charolais

POSITION	CREW	CALL	POSITION	CREW	CALL
1st AD	Michael Stanton		Dolly Grip		
Cinematographer	Katherine Williams	9:00	Sound Mixer		
1st AC			Boom Op	Javier Martinez	
Gaffer		10:00	Makeup/Hair	-	
Key Grip	-		Script Super		

#	CAST	CHARACTER	PU	MU/HAIR	SET	NOTES
1	Yoel Martinez	YOEL	9:30			SELF DRIVE
2	Juliette Guerrault	JULIETTE	9:30			SELF DRIVE
3	Maria Aparicio	WAITRESS	9:30			

#	EXTRAS/ATMOSPHERE	CALL	SPECIAL REQUIREMENTS

MISCELLANEOUS AND SPECIAL INSTRUCTIONS

LOCATION
1805 W State of Franklin Rd #1200, Johnson City, TN 37604

Director Phone Number 646 918 4967

Figure 13. Call Sheet

THE OTHER

Production

The main technical issues that we had that date were some low batteries and noises coming from the kitchen, but overall, the production for this film was smooth and good. The owner of El Charolais restaurant let us shoot there during the period in which they set up the tables for the day, early in the morning. We spent a few hours in the restaurant shooting and afterwards, I invited the crew and cast to eat in the same restaurant.

Although I had checked out the Blackmagic camera, the cinematographer preferred to use her own gear, a Canon Rebel T5, and the result was really good. The audio had some noise issues but it was acceptable. The audio was recorded separately, so a slate was used to keep track of the shots and to be able to synchronize the audio and the shots (see Figure 14 and 15.)

Figure 14. Production Day (Photo Credit: Katherine Williams)

Figure 15. "The Blind Date" Still

Postproduction

The postproduction step for this film was easier than the other two, since this film has a linear plot and did not have special effects. However, this one was the first film for project in which audio was recorded. It was recorded in a separate way by means of using the Zoom Audio Recorded and the Boom Microphone. In postproduction, it was important to synchronize the audio files with the video files correctly, which took a few hours. Once synched, I could start to edit the rough cut.

One of the biggest challenges of editing this film was finding the right music. Fortunately, I found the perfect song in Jamendo, a website with Creative Commons music: a song with Bachata rhythm and French lyrics, which would combine the music for my film.

Film IV. "The Show"

Preproduction

This film is a fiction film and the plot is about the making of a Telenovela or TV show. The way in which ethnic groups are depicted in this kind of shows were the starting point of my thesis project, so I had to include at least one film that had these shows as the main theme.

In this film, a TV show´s crew and cast are in the middle of producing an episode, when one of the actors starts to question his role as a Latino drug dealer; he would like to be portrayed in a different light, in more favorable roles such as businessman, etc. The script for this film, and specially the dialogue in which the actor is questioning the industry´s stereotypes was really important for me, since it meant giving the characters the lines that I would myself like to hear in an effort for a change. The script required several edits to sound less preachy, but I was satisfied with the final result (see Figure 16.)

```
                              JOSE
               Julya, I don't know. It just
               doesn't feel good anymore.

                            DIRECTOR
               What do you mean?

                              JOSE
               You know... The Latino drug dealer, Maria and the baby...

                            DIRECTOR
               Why does this matter now? You have thousands of fans, you're
               making lots of money...

                              JOSE
               We could make something else, you know. Something different.

                            DIRECTOR
               This is what sells and you knew this when we started. What do you
               want? Do you want to be a Latino businessman? Who would watch our
               show? Nobody wants to see that. The Audience wants something more
               exciting, they want to see a Latin Lover like you... (Reaches to
               touch his cheek)

                              JOSE
               (Backs up)
               I'm serious. I know I can do different roles. I'm a good actor.

                            DIRECTOR
               Of course you are.

                              JOSE
               It's just... I'm tired of this.
```

Figure 16: "The Show" Script Excerpt

The rented equipment for this film was the Blackmagic camera, an HTC camera for the second perspective, the Zoom Audio Recorded and Boom Microphone, light reflector, and a dolly. The location was the studio at the RTVF department, in order to use the green screen. In order to rent the studio, I had to submit the proper forms and give notice to Public Safety on campus that we would be shooting inside the building on a Saturday.

Production

The production for this film was good, we were for the first time a big group of people: 5 talents and 4 Crew members. Together, we pulled together a Dolly shot of which I'm really proud of, but that took several takes. I wanted to have a long shot with no cuts for the very first scene, so it had to be perfect.

Another one of the challenges was that it was cold, but the scene we were shooting was to be set by the sea (thanks to the green screen), so the actors kept wearing and taking off their coats (see Figure 17.) This produced some continuity issues that we had to keep in mind the whole time. However, overall the production was good, we had a break to eat pizza, we recorded everything in a full day and we had amazing footage with the Dolly shot.

Figure 17: Production of "The Show" (Film Still)

In the second scene of the film, the private conversation between the Director and the main actor that I have mentioned, there is a Caution sign in the background (see Figure 18.) This sign could have been avoided, since there was plenty of room. However, I chose to include it in the frame, as a symbol of how the words that the actor is saying represent a danger to the film industry, which is so conditioned by stereotypes.

Figure 18: Caution sign (Film Still)

Postproduction

The postproduction for this film was long and exhausting. I also spent a few hours synching the audio and the video, since we recorded separately. However, this is the best strategy to record audio in film production. I fount the music once again in Jamendo, a song with drums and fast paced rhythm that would represent the production fast rhythm.

The main goal of recording in the studio and using the green screen was to be able to edit the background and have the characters play a scene in the beach, to later change it for a more sophisticated location for the last scene (see Figure 19.) Working with the green screen was hard, since it was my first time and I had some lighting issues that made the keying complicated. However, after some hard work and great help from Daniel Santiago at the RTVF department, I was able to fix the issues and have a good Chroma keying. The final duration of the film is 6 minutes.

Figure 19: Chroma Keying for "The Show"

Film V: "The Other"

Preproduction

The final film for this thesis project is a documentary about the project itself and the reactions of the audiences after watching the films that make part of the project. Since this was going to be the final film, it had to be the one that would bring the conclusion of my project and would bring the discussion back to social research, through interviews. As it is a documentary, there was no written script; but a general design of how this film would be laid out.

- Introduction to the project and the films, a brief making-of.
- Interviews to random students on campus about stereotypes in film and TV.
- Audience's reaction after a screening of the films and discussion.

In order to get the necessary footage for the third section and to have an idea of what the perception of the films would be for an audience, I organized a public film screening in collaboration with International Student Association. A flyer was made and posted throughout campus and social media (see Figure 20.)

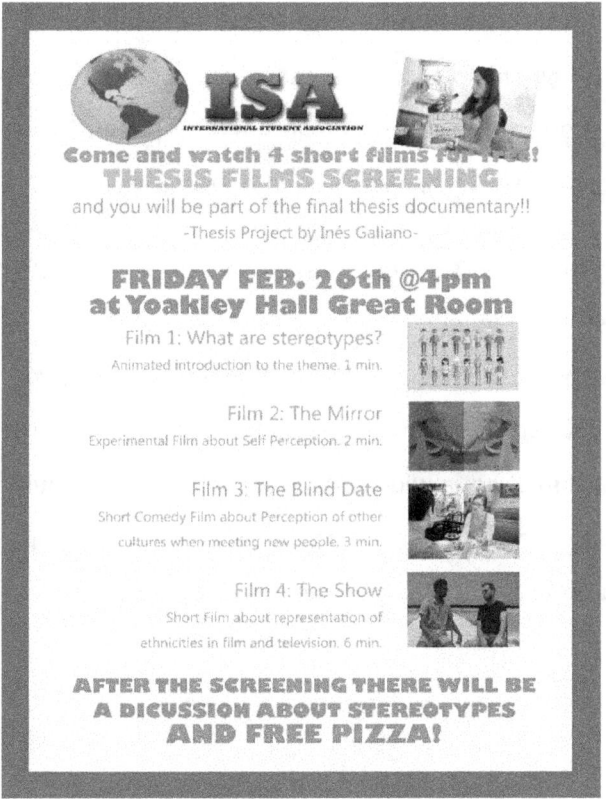

Figure 20: Flyer for the Screening of the Films

Production

The main focus for the production of this film was to get interviews from people on campus, and get footage from the screening event. For the interviews, I asked some random students with the only prerequisite that they had to be from the dominating ethnicity, so that we could see their point of view and their reaction to the films and input on the topic.

For the interviews segment, I asked some people to watch some of the films from my laptop and talk about their perceptions and impact. Finally, for the screening, I had two cameras to get two points of view; a stationary camera in the back of the room to get a wide shot, and someone that could help as videographer to get individual close ups on the people that spoke during the discussion time (see Figure 21.)

Figure 21: Screening of the films and stereotypes presentation
(Photo Credit: Yohann Aboa)

Postproduction

The postproduction challenges that I faced editing this film were the amount of footage I had from the interviews. The main steps where to reduce he amount of footage to an acceptable amount and to keep the most important lines that my interviewees said.

Finding the right music that would set the tone of the documentary was also one of the hardest things, but I found creative commons songs in Jamendo once again. I chose a more vivid song for the making of segment and a slower one for the interviews segment. The final duration of the documentary is around 12 minutes.

CHAPTER 5

CONCLUSION

When I started this thesis project I set myself certain goals and objectives related to my research on stereotypes, to my filmmaking skills and to understand who I am as a filmmaker. Now, reflecting upon the whole projects, I think I met most of my goals and I learned so much.

Developing My Research

The first and primary goal of this thesis project was to further develop my research on stereotypes, by creating a series of films around that same topic. From exploring the issues that people face when dealing with stereotypes set by the media, to understanding how people react when confronted with the subject, and looking for a common solution for the problem; I now have a better understanding of the whole situation.

I started by researching if these mediated ethnic stereotypes affected the audience's perception of that stereotyped ethnic or cultural group, and found from my interviewees' reactions that they do affect the audience. However, there is not a single or easy solution to the problem, since we are so conditioned and used to this kind of representations to the point that even the people from those groups will believe that they are that way.

One of the possible solutions that we could enforce to solve this problems is making an effort for hiring a more diverse casting when making films or producing TV shows; having not only white people in the place of the heroes of the story, and not only other ethnicities in the secondary or villain roles. We are starting to see some media makers and companies that support ethnicities by creating innovative media such as Netflix, etc. Hopefully, these companies will keep working towards a more inclusive Film and TV industry.

Another solution in the casting domain could be not having ethnic characters at all, or casting non-characters in the roles that are usually played by different ethnicities. However, it will not be enough with hiring more ethnicities in small roles that have no impact on the industry whereas is in the cast or in the crew. We need other ethnicities to be writers and directors, as well as producers; we need them to tell their stories.

However, we must not forget that the film and TV industry is driven by profit, as well as every other industry. Thus, the only way to put pressure on the producers and the heads of the industry is to support a certain product or not as the customer. It is the customer's right to choose what product to buy, so it is only fair that if we want to see some change, we need to buy, rent, and watch films and shows that are progressive and freed from stereotyped ethnic roles. We can also help by doing the opposite, by not buying tickets or watching the films and shows that portray ethnicities in the traditional and stereotyped way. This is something that we can easily do to help support the creation of new representations, and, in my opinion, the most efficient way to do it, since films and shows are always made for an audience. If we all make an effort and follow this measure, things can and will certainly change.

Learning about Myself as a Filmmaker and Exploring the Issue from the Inside

The second goal of my thesis project was to learn about myself as a filmmaker by stepping out of my comfort zone and making a series of films with different genres, as well as developing my filmmaking skills at the same time and explore the issue from the inside of the industry itself. When I first started with this project, my knowledge and production skills were rather limited. However, I can say that working hard and trying to do my best in all five of these films has certainly made an impact on me and has made me and my abilities grow.

The genres that I explored were animation, experimental, skit, fiction and documentary; and all of them have been a challenge for different reasons. The animation film made me gain some technical computer skills that I will certainly use in the future. The experimental film, being maybe the hardest one to accomplish, has taught me how to develop a complex and abstract concept and try to represent it through images and sound. The skit and the fiction film were certainly a learning experience about the whole filmmaking industry and gave me valuable production skills that I will use in my future career. And finally, the documentary made me look into the issue from the human side, forcing me to reconnect with the world once again and with the audiences, learning from them as they learned from my films.

Addressing Stereotypes via filmmaking has given me some virtues and limitations, like any other approach would have. The main two virtues that this approach offered me is that it is a more empirical and hands on option, and I could express much through it, and that I have been able to explore the issue from its root. To analyze media, we must understand media, and trying to produce media was the best approach for me to understand it and analyze it.

This approach also has some limitations, including that it may not always be as direct as other approaches and that it may not be as generalizable. However, it has been a starting to point to look at the issue that can lead to future paths, for example, by screening the films in front of more varied audiences and doing more social research based on their reactions and ideas.

Limitations, Progress and Future

In this section I wish to address and acknowledge the limitations, mistakes and lessons learned that arose during the creation and a posteriori reflection. The main issue during the production of these 5 films was the challenge on getting the resources that I needed. For instance, I could not always get the help, support and crewmembers needed for the production days. In most of the films, the crew is very small, resulting in small mistakes that could have been avoided, such as not having all the actors prepared for audio recording.

It is also important to consider for the future that every choice made during production will be relevant to the final product. For the most part, I chose certain things like the music, the colors, or the locations, for a purpose, with an idea in mind. However, this has not always been the case, since availability and convenience were also important.

Another lesson I will take for my future projects will be to further develop the relation between my films. Although the main link between these films is the topic, they could have had a stronger linking element to them. Also, thinking and preparing a distribution plan for the films could have helped in the production as well: it is very different the formats that will be acceptable for online platforms such as YouTube than the format for a Gallery screening, for example.

Another important issue that could have developed my

project could have been to include in my preproduction research some articles written from the Filmmaking standpoint. This is not always easy, since such a thing is not common. However, a section addressing the current trend of innovative media and efforts for changing the issue from the Filmmaking standpoint could have helped transition between my research and the production. With no doubt, such a chapter will be something that I will probably develop in the future.

Finally, reflecting on this idea of finding the best place or medium for my films, I find that The Mirror, The Blind Date and The Show could stand alone and be presented at festivals. However, the first film and the final documentary have the goal of introducing and giving a conclusion to the project as a whole, so they would have to be seen in context with the other films. Considering the main goal of this project -to make a change in the issue of ethnic representations-, an ideal place for screening the films would be a community environment outside the university setting. The university setting provides an environment of discussion that it is very convenient for the project. However, for the purpose of rising awareness, it would be more beneficial to screen the films outside the school, and to find an audience that can be less aware of the situation.

INÉS GALIANO

Final Thoughts

While making all five of these films, I have grown as a filmmaker and I have created a body of work that I will be able to show and send to festivals, as well as being useful as a portfolio for future projects and possible jobs later in life. I have discovered a complete new industry for me and I have found that I love it, and that I want to keep working to improve myself and my skills to find my place in it.

I have also learned that there is not one single solution, but many, and that we can all contribute and collaborate to change this important issue, and give more opportunities for other ethnicities to tell their stories without being stereotyped and marginalized. I have learned that in filmmaking, creating drama and engaging the audience is one of the main goals, and that trying to do that while trying to be socially conscious is a challenge, but not impossible. These are important times for starting the conversation in a more and more diverse society, and this thesis project is adding to the conversation from a different perspective.

This project can be used to further develop the research on

ethnic representations, as well as join a combined effort to change them. The 5 films will hopefully be screened in the future, through public screenings or through online platforms such as YouTube or Vimeo, contributing to the goal of raising awareness about the issue, developing new strategies and triggering future research.

INÉS GALIANO

BIBLIOGRAPHY

Avila-Saavedra, Guillermo. "Ethnic Otherness Versus Cultural

Assimilation: U.S. Latino Comedians And The Politics Of

Identity." *Mass Communication & Society* 14.3 (2011): 271-

291

Galiano-Torres, Ines. "Audience´s Perception of Cultural/Ethnic

Stereotypes in TV Shows". *European Scientific Journal*

(2015):1-15

Guo, Lei, and Summer Harlow. "User-Generated Racism: An

Analysis Of Stereotypes Of African Americans, Latinos, And

Asians In Youtube Videos." *Howard Journal Of*

Communications 25.3 (2014): 281-302.

Halse, Rolf. "Negotiating Boundaries Between Us and

Them." *NORDICOM Review* 33.1   (2012): 37-52.

Igartua, Juan-José, Isabel M. Barrios, and Félix Ortega.

"Analysis of the Image of Immigration in Prime Time

Television Fiction." *Comunicación y Sociedad* 25.2

(2012): 5-28.

Inzunza Acedo, Beatriz E. "Recepción de Estereotipos de la Serie

Norteamericana Lost Entre Jóvenes que Habitan En

Monterrey, México. (Spanish)." *Signo y Pensamiento* 32.62

(2013): 16-31.

Lee, Moon J., et al. "Television Viewing and Ethnic Stereotypes:

Do College Students Form Stereotypical Perceptions of

Ethnic Groups as a Result of Heavy Television

Consumption?." *Howard Journal of Communications* 20.1

(2009): 95-110.

Mastro, Dana E., and Elizabeth Behm-Morazwitz. "Latino

Representation on Primetime Television."

Journalism & Mass Communication Quarterly 82.1

(2005): 110-130.

Mastro, Dana, and Riva Tukachinsky. "The Influence Of Exemplar

   Versus Prototype-Based Media Primes On Racial/Ethnic

   Evaluations."*Journal Of Communication* 61.5 (2011): 916-

   937.

Merskin, Debra. "Three Faces of Eva: Perpetuation of the Hot-

   Latina Stereotype in Desperate Housewives." *Howard*

   Journal of Communications 18.2 (2007): 133-151.

Murillo Sandoval, Sandra Leticia, and Luis Escala Rabadán.

   "Fealdad, Alteridad Y Representación De La Población

   Latina En Estados Unidos En El Discurso Televisivo De   Ugly

   Betty. (Spanish)." *Comunicación Y Sociedad (0188-252X)* 20

   (2013): 113-134.

Northup, Temple. "Is Everyone a Little Bit Racist?

   Exploring Cultivation Using Implicit and Explicit

   Measures."*Southwestern Mass Communication*

   Journal 26.1 (2010): 29-41.

Ramasubramanian, Srividya. "Television Viewing, Racial

Attitudes, and Policy Preferences: Exploring the Role of

Social Identity and Intergroup Emotions in Influencing

Support for Affirmative Action." *Communication*

Monographs 77.1 (2010): 102-120.

Sanders, Meghan S., and Srividya Ramasubramanian.

"An Examination of African Americans' Stereotyped

Perceptions of Fictional Media Characters." *Howard*

Journal of Communications 23.1 (2012): 17-39.

Washington, Myra. "Interracial Intimacy: Hegemonic

Construction Of Asian American And Black Relationships On

TV Medical Dramas."*Howard Journal Of*

Communications 23.3 (2012): 253- 271.

Zhang, Qin. "Asian Americans Beyond the Model

Minority Stereotype: The Nerdy and the Left

Out." *Journal of International & Intercultural*

THE OTHER

Communication 3.1 (2010): 20-37.

INÉS GALIANO

APPENDICES

Appendix A: Script of "The Blind Date"

<3.07

OR

The Blind Date>

by

<Inés Galiano>

INÉS GALIANO

INT. - DAY - RESTAURANT

WIDE SHOT OF GIRL SITTING ALONE AT A TABLE IN A
RESTAURANT. SHE IS WEARING AN ELEGANT DRESS AND
SHE SEEMS TO BE WAITING FOR SOMETHING. WAITRESS
APPROACHES HER.

WAITRESS

What can I get for you?

JULIETTE

Oh, sorry, I´m waiting for someone. I have a
blind date.

WAITRESS

Alright.

(Look to the side, not believing)

Suddenly, Juliette sees him going up the hill.
Shot of him in slow motion with epic music. Yoel
gets there. Juliette gets up.

THE OTHER

JULIETTE

Jose?

YOEL

No.

JULIETTE

Antonio?

YOEL

No.

JULIETTE

Yoel!

YOEL

Yes. Juliette?

JULIETTE

Si!

He smiles and sits in front of her.

YOEL

Bonjour.

JULIETTE

Hola.

Waitress suddenly again appears between them

WAITRESS

What can I get for you?

They split suddenly, embarrassed.

YOEL

Cavernet Sauvignon.

JULIETTE

Cerveza Modelo.

Waitress writes quickly and disappears.

They look at each other. They are nervous,
trying not to look at each other.

JULIETTE

THE OTHER

So... what type of music do you like?

YOEL

I love Piaf, Edith Piaf.

JULIETTE

Oh wow... one of the classics..

YOEL

And you?

JULIETTE

I love Enrique Iglesias!

YOEL

Great...

YOEL

How about movies?

JULIETTE

The Mask of Zorro.

YOEL

Amelie.

JULIETTE

INÉS GALIANO

Books?

YOEL

Les Miserables.

JULIETTE

Love in time of Cholera.

They look at each other, as if they had found
their soul mate. Waitress appears out of
nowhere, with the drinks. They separate quickly.

WAITRESS

Something to eat?

JULIETTE

Nachos.

YOEL

Brie Cheese.

WAITRES

(She makes a face)

Ok...

THE OTHER

They take their drinks up for a toast.

YOEL

For love.

JULIETTE

For love is life.

YOEL

For love is grand.

(Tension moment.)

Nachos appear in between them.

WAITRESS

And divorce is a hundred grand.

JULIETTE

Excuse me?

WAITRESS

Would you like something else?

YOEL

Actually, could we have some dance music?

WAITRESS

Sure...

(And disappears.)

Romantic Music starts playing.

YOEL

Would you like to dance?

JULIETTE

Yes.

He takes her hand, they start dancing slowly.

YOEL

Do you surrender?

JULIETTE

Never, but I may scream.

YOEL

I understand. I sometimes have that effect.

THE OTHER

WAITRESS

Is there anything else I can get for you?

YOEL

The lady and I were trying to dance.

WAITRESS

You were trying. She was succeeding.

YOEL

Excuse me?

WAITRESS

Do you want the check together or separate?

YOEL

Together.

JULIETTE

Separate.

The waitress brings the check. They sit back in
the bench to look at the paper. They hold hands.

YOEL

When can I see you again? How long are you here for?

JULIETTE

I live here.

YOEL

Great! Me too.

JULIETTE

Don´t you miss your family?

YOEL

Yes, but you know, I visit some weekends. But It must be harder for you.

JULIETTE

It´s fine. I see them every two weeks.

YOEL

Wait. You go to France every two weeks?

JULIETTE

To France? I´m from Ohio.

YOEL

Seriously?

THE OTHER

JULIETTE

You are from Mexico, right?

YOEL

I´m from Illinois.

JULIETTE

You lied to me!

YOEL

You never asked me that!

They look at each other, awkwardly. They stop
holding hands. They get up.

JULIETTE

Ok. It was nice to meet you, but

I am pretty busy.

YOEL

Yes, I have things to do today.

I´ll see you soon.

JULIETTE

INÉS GALIANO

I´ll be busy.

YOEL

Ok.

JULIETTE

Goodbye.

YOEL

Bye.

The waitress comes to the table, sits and starts drinking the beer while looking at them. For love. CU of nachos and cheese.

FADE OUT

THE OTHER

Appendix B: Script of "The Show"

```
<THE SHOW>


        by


<INES GALIANO>
```

INT. - DAY - STUDIO

STUDIO. ACTORS AND CREW ARE PREPARING FOR
SHOOTING A SCENE WITH THE GREEN SCREEN.

SHOT OF A CHARACTER BRINGING COFEE TO A TABLE,
WHERE THE DIRECTOR IS TALKING TO THE AD

DIRECTOR

We´ll start with the 2 shot with the dialogue
about the money, and then we´ll go to close-ups.

AD

(Taking note)

Ok, if we manage to get the scene done by noon,
we´ll save up a lot on budget.

DIRECTOR

I don´t want to lose the Insert shots this time,
so I´m not sure about that.

AD

I´ll see if we can start.

(Leaves to talk to the crew)

SHOT FOLLOWING THE DIRECTOR TOWARDS THE GREEN
SCREEN, WHERE THE ACTORS ARE SEATING ON CHAIRS,
wearing coats.

THE OTHER

DIRECTOR

How are you guys feeling today?

JOSE

I didn´t sleep really good, actually.

RAPHA

I´m fine, I slept like a baby.

DIRECTOR

You will do great. We are starting in about 5
minutes, alright?

RAPHA

Alright. Just to make sure. Do we have a beach
behind us?

DIRECTOR

No, no, you are in the porch of a cabana.

We´ll add the background in post.

RAPHA

Alright!

SHOT FOLLOWING THE DIRECTOR WALKING TO HER SPOT
NEXT TO THE CAMERAPERSON, WHO IS ADJUSTING THE
FOCUS.

THE ACTORS TAKE THE COATS OFF.

AD

Alright, everyone´s ready?

Quiet on set!

(Uses the slate in front of the camera)

Scene 5 take 1 roll 1

DIRECTOR

And... Action.

2 SHOT OF THE ACTORS WITH ONLY GREEN CREEN
BEHIND

JOSE

Did you bring what I asked?

RAPHA

Yeah. It´s on the bag.

JOSE

Show me.

THE OTHER

RAPHA

Wait. It´s not going to be that easy. I want to
see the merchandise first.

JOSE

You´ll have it after you give me the money.

They look at each other.

RAPHA

I talked to Maria.

JOSE

(Surprised)

To Maria? Have you seen Maria?

Phone rings and the actors look surprised to the
camera.

DIRECTOR

Cut! Didn´t you turn off your phone?

(Looking angrily at the AD)

ACTORS PUT COATS BACK ON, AS IF FREEZING.

AD

(Apologetically, looking for the phone
everyehwere)

INÉS GALIANO

I thought so...

DIRECTOR

(Makes face and goes to talk to the actors)

You are clear on what you´re doing, right?

JOSE

(Tired)

I´m a drugdealer, whose objective is to steal
from this guy.[Jose is tired of playing the
stereotype]

DIRECTOR

Yes, but remember why. You need to protect your
family. Getting the money now could mean that
your family is safe from now on. You´re
desperate. And you... (Looking at Rapha), you
want to get the best deal here, and you´re going
to play your cards.

AD

We´re ready now.

ACTORS TAKE COATS BACK OFF.

AD

Everyone´s ready? Scene 5, take 2 roll 1.

DIRECTOR

THE OTHER

And... Action!

RAPHA

I talked to Maria.

JOSE

(Emotive) Maria? You saw her?

RAPHA

Yes, I see her often.

JOSE

How is she? (Really emotive)

RAPHA

She´s good, working at a hotel. The baby is good too. Already talks some. He´s almost two, you know.

JOSE

I wish I could... (Breaks)

There is an uncomfortable silence, because Jose has forgotten the lines. Rapha is looking confused.

RAPHA

You wish you could...?

JOSE

INÉS GALIANO

Hmmm. You know, I wish I could...

DIRECTOR

Alright, Cut! Let´s take 5 minutes break.

AD

You sure? We are already behind schedule...

DIRECTOR

I´m sure (angry)

AD

Alright, everybody! 5 minutes break!

DIRECTOR

JOSE, let´s walk out for a minute.

They leave.

RAPHA

What´s for lunch?

TRANSITION

SHOT OF DIRECTOR AND JOSE IN ANOTHER ROOM

DIRECTOR

What´s troubling you...

THE OTHER

JOSE

Julya, I don't know. It just

doesn't feel good anymore.

DIRECTOR

What do you mean?

JOSE

You know... The Latino drug dealer, Maria and
the baby...

DIRECTOR

Why does this matter now? You have thousands of
fans, you're making lots of money...

JOSE

We could make something else, you know.
Something different.

DIRECTOR

This is what sells and you knew this when we
started. What do you want? Do you want to be a
Latino businessman? Who would watch our show?
Nobody wants to see that. The Audience wants
something more exciting; they want to see a
Latin Lover like you... (Reaches to touch his
cheek)

JOSE

(Backs up)

I´m serious. I know I can do different roles.
I´m a good actor.

DIRECTOR

Of course you are.

JOSE

It´s just... I´m tired of this.

DIRECTOR

There's nothing we can do about it…

JOSE

(Looks at her, with hope) Yes! There is! A
latino businessman!

DIRECTOR

What? Seriously?

JOSE

Yes, let´s do it!

Or a lawyer! Or a judge! (Dreamingly, happy)

DIRECTOR

THE OTHER

It would be like starting over...

JOSE

We´ll give Maria another job. She can be a
senator.

DIRECTOR

(Thinking) That could actually work...

JOSE

(Holds her hand) It will work. Trust me. We can
change this.

TRANSITION

SHOT FOLLOWING THE DIRECTOR TOWARDS THE GREEN
SCREEN, WHERE THE ACTORS ARE SEATING ON CHAIRS.
This time the actors are dressed in
suits/formally.

DIRECTOR

You guys ready?

RAPHA

You bet. Just to make sure: Do we have congress
behind us?

DIRECTOR

INÉS GALIANO

No, no, you are in the oval office.

RAPHA

Alright!

SHOT FOLLOWING THE DIRECTOR WALKING TO HER SPOT NEXT TO THE CAMERAPERSON, WHO IS ADJUSTING THE FOCUS.

AD

Alright, everyone´s ready? Quiet on set!

(Uses the slate in front of the camera)

Scene 5 take 1 roll 1

DIRECTOR

And... Action.

2 SHOT OF THE ACTORS WITH ONLY GREEN CREEN BEHIND

JOSE

Did you bring what I asked?

RAPHA

Yeah. It´s on the bag.

JOSE

THE OTHER

Show me.

RAPHA

Wait. It´s not going to be that easy. I need to
read the brief first.

JOSE

You´ll have it after you tell my why you went
through with the negotiations. I said we
wouldn´t talk with the consulate until they
opened their borders.

They look at each other.

RAPHA

I talked to Maria.

JOSE

(Surprised)

To Maria? Have you seen Maria? I thought she was
at the United Nations until tomorrow?

Phone rings and the actors look surprised to the
camera.

DIRECTOR

Cut! Didn´t you turn off your phone?

(Looking angrily at the AD)

AD

I´m sorry...

FADE OUT

THE END

THE OTHER

VITA

INÉS GALIANO TORRES

Education:

M.A. in Professional Communication, East Tennessee State
University, Johnson City, Tennessee, 2016

Graduate Certificate in Healthcare Translation and Interpreting,
East Tennessee State University, Johnson City, Tennessee,
2015

B.A. Translation and Interpreting, University of Murcia, Murcia
Spain 2014

Professional Experience:

Production Intern for the live show Daytime Tri-cities at WJHL,
Johnson City, Tennessee, 2015

Editor for the magazine *El Nuevo Tennessean,* East Tennessee
State University, Johnson City, Tennessee, 2014-2015

Production Intern, Mary B Martin School of the Arts, East
Tennessee State University, Johnson City, Tennessee, 2015

INÉS GALIANO

Graduate Assistant, Language and Culture Resource Center, East Tennessee State University, Johnson City, Tennessee, 2014-2016

Academic talks:

Audience´s Perception of Cultural/Ethnic Stereotypes in TV Shows at the 3rd Mediterranean Interdisciplinary Forum, Barcelona, Spain, June 2015

Audience´s Perception of Cultural/Ethnic Stereotypes in TV Shows at the Appalachian Student Research Forum March 2015

Academic publications:

Audience´s Perception of Cultural/Ethnic Stereotypes in TV Shows at the European Scientific Journal, July 2015

Senior Undergraduate Thesis: *"La traducción de la manera y su impacto en la audiencia meta: un studio de recepción".* University of Murcia, Spain, June 2014.

THE OTHER

Published Books:

Who is Sara Marst?, Createspace, 2015

Paella y Fish and Chips, A play, Createspace, 2014

The Forest's Edge, Createspace, 2013

30 days, Createspace, 2013

Departure, Createspace, 2012

Films:

The Other, A documentary, Johnson City, Tennessee, 2016

The Show, Johnson City, Tennessee, 2015

The Blind Date, Johnson City, Tennessee, 2015

The Mirror, Johnson City, Tennessee, 2015

What are Stereotypes? , Johnson City, Tennessee, 2015

Frames, Johnson City, Tennessee, 2015

Light and Shadows, Prague, Czech Republic, 2015

INÉS GALIANO

One heart, A short documentary, Johnson City, Tennessee, 2015

The Nature of Documentary, Co-directed with Ophelie Fuxa,

Johnson City, Tennessee, 2015

Awards:

Outstanding Graduate Creative Achievement at East Tennessee
State University for the Masters final thesis project, April
2016.

Outstanding Contribution by Graduate Student at East
Tennessee   State University for the work with *El Nuevo*
Tennessean, April 2016

The Innovation Award by Quantum Ascension Studios and East
Tennessee State University for the film *Frames,* April
2016.

Best Director at Direct Short & Documentary Film Festival July
2015 for the film *Light and Shadows.*

Audience Award for Best Director at Prague Film School Summer

Workshop 2015 for the film *Light and Shadows.*

WATCH THE FILMS

DVD Available in Amazon

Streaming available in Vimeo
https://vimeo.com/album/3882069

Check the author's website: http://inesgaliano.com/

www.ingramcontent.com/pod-product-compliance
Lightning Source LLC
Chambersburg PA
CBHW072200280526
45788CB00002B/818